V Tı RECIPES

Traditional home-made favourites including cakes, buns, breads and biscuits

SALMON

Index

Almond Buns   14
Angel Cake   35
Apple Cake   6
Banana Teabread   11
Boiled Cake   32
Butterscotch Brownies   47
Cheese Scones   15
Chocolate Cookies   10
Coconut and Cherry Cake   31
Coffee and Walnut Rock Buns   7
Crispy Coconut Cookies   26
Custard Tarts   46
Dundee Cake   40
Drop Scones   19
Fruited Scones   29
Ginger and Raisin Cake   18
Gingerbread   21

Honey Cake with Ginger   21
Lemon Biscuits   37
Lemon Cake   24
Macaroons   8
Marmalade Cake   38
Meringues   45
Oat Crunchies   42
Plain Buns   22
Plain Scones   14
Rich Malt Loaf   16
Rich Seed Cake   34
Ring Doughnuts   39
Rock Cakes   43
Shortbread   27
Strawberry Shortcake   5
Sultana Cake   30
Victoria Sandwich   3

Printed and published by J. Salmon Ltd., Sevenoaks, England © Copyright
Title page photograph: ALAMY

Victoria Sandwich

6 oz. self-raising flour   6 oz. butter
6 oz. caster sugar   2 tbsp. jam
3 eggs, beaten

Butter two 7 inch sandwich tins and line the base of each with buttered greaseproof paper. Beat the butter and sugar together and add the eggs a little at a time, mixing in well after each addition. Gradually fold in the flour. Divide the mixture between each tin and spread with a knife. Bake in the oven at 375°F or Gas mark 5 for about 20 minutes, until they are well risen and firm to the touch. Turn out and cool on a wire rack. When the cakes are cool, sandwich them together with a layer of jam to taste and sprinkle the top with caster sugar.

Strawberry Shortcake

8 oz. flour	4 oz. butter
3 level tsp. baking powder	7 fl.oz. milk
1-1½ lb. strawberries	5 fl.oz. double cream
¼ level tsp. salt	Icing sugar
2 oz. caster sugar	

Set aside six strawberries and mash the rest in a bowl. Grease two 8 inch sandwich tins. Sift the flour, baking powder and salt into a bowl. Stir in the caster sugar and rub in 3 oz. of the butter to give a coarse consistency. Add the milk and mix until blended. Divide the dough between the two tins, spread level, then dot with the remaining butter. Bake in the oven at 450°F or Gas mark 8 for about 12 minutes, until well risen, golden and firm to the touch. Turn out and cool on a cake rack. Whip the fresh cream until stiff. Place one shortcake upside down on a plate, cover with a layer of whipped fresh cream then the crushed strawberries. Top with the other shortcake, the right side up, spread more cream on top and decorate with the whole strawberries.

Apple Cake

8 oz. self-raising flour   1 tsp. salt   4 oz. butter
1 lb. cooking or dessert apples, peeled, cored and chopped
4 oz. caster sugar   2 eggs, beaten   1 oz. soft brown sugar

Sift the flour and salt into a mixing bowl. Cut the butter into the flour and rub in to a breadcrumb consistency. Mix in the apples, caster sugar and eggs. Turn into a greased 8 inch cake tin. Smooth off the top and sprinkle with the brown sugar. Bake in a preheated moderately hot oven at 400°F or Gas mark 6 for 30 to 40 minutes. Allow to cool slightly before turning out. Serve hot with cream, or if eating cold, cool on a wire tray and serve with butter.

Coffee and Walnut Rock Buns

4 oz. flour	2 oz. walnuts, chopped
4 oz. wholemeal flour	3 oz. soft brown sugar
4 oz. butter	1 egg
2 tsp. baking powder	2 tbsp. coffee essence
Pinch of salt	Milk

Sift the two flours, salt and baking powder into a mixing bowl. Cut the butter into the flour and rub in to a breadcrumb consistency. Mix in the sugar and chopped nuts. Beat the egg and coffee essence together, then stir into the mixture adding sufficient milk to give a stiff dough. Using a fork heap the mixture into rocky mounds on a greased baking sheet. Bake near the top of a preheated moderately hot oven at 400°F or Gas mark 6 for 15 to 20 minutes. Remove from the sheet and cool on a wire tray.

Macaroons

4 oz. caster sugar	4 oz. ground almonds
1 tsp. ground rice	Almond essence
2 egg whites	Halved almonds

Add the sugar, ground almonds and ground rice to a bowl and gradually beat in the egg whites and a few drops of almond essence until the mixture is of a soft consistency. Place in a piping bag fitted with a ½ inch plain tube. Pipe the mixture into 2 inch circles on rice paper placed on baking sheets. Press a halved almond into each macaroon. Bake in a moderate oven 325°F or Gas mark 3 for 15 to 20 minutes. Using a palette knife, cut out and place the macaroons on a wire tray to cool.

Chocolate Cookies

5 oz. self-raising flour	**2 oz. fine semolina**
8 oz. butter	**3 oz. icing sugar**
2 oz. cornflour	**4 oz. plain chocolate, melted**

Grease 18 madeleine moulds. Sift the flour, semolina and cornflour into a bowl. Whisk the butter and icing sugar together until fluffy. Stir in the flour mixture to form a soft paste. Press a little of the mixture into each mould and level the top. Bake in the oven at 350°F or Gas mark 4 for 15 to 20 minutes. Leave to cool a little in the tins before gently easing out. When cold, dredge with icing sugar and dip the ends of each cookie in melted chocolate.

Banana Teabread

8 oz. self-raising flour	1 lb. ripe bananas
6 oz. caster sugar	Grated rind of one lemon
4 oz. butter	2 oz. glacé cherries, chopped
2 eggs	4 oz. raisins

Mash the bananas, reserving a whole one for decoration. Place all the ingredients in a food processor and beat slowly until well mixed. Place in a 2 lb. greased and lined loaf tin. Bake in a moderate oven 325°F or Gas mark 3 for 1½ to 1¾ hours. Turn out and cool on a wire tray. Decorate with the reserved banana cut into slices and dipped in lemon juice to prevent discolouration. To serve, slice and spread with butter.

Plain Scones

8 oz. flour   ½ tsp. salt   4 tsp. baking powder
1-2 oz. butter   ¼ pint milk

Heat the oven to 450°F or Gas mark 8, and warm a baking sheet. Sift the flour, salt and baking powder into a mixing bowl. Cut the butter into the flour and rub in to a breadcrumb consistency. Make a well in the centre, pour in the milk and mix into a soft spongy dough, adding a little water if necessary. Turn the dough out on to a floured board and knead lightly. Roll out the dough with a floured rolling pin until ¾ inch thick. Cut into rounds with a 2½ inch floured pastry cutter. Place on the baking sheet. Shape the remaining dough into a ball and flatten into a circle, cut into quarters and place on the baking sheet. Brush the scones with milk for a glazed finish or rub with flour for a soft crust. Bake near the top of the hot oven for 7 to 10 minutes until well risen and golden on top.

Almond Buns

6 oz. flour **½ tsp. baking powder** **Salt**
3 oz. butter **2 oz. caster sugar** **1 egg, beaten**
2 oz. ground almonds **1 oz. caster sugar** **1 oz. icing sugar**
1 egg, separated **Lemon juice**

Sift the flour, baking powder and salt into a bowl. Cut the butter into the flour and rub in to a breadcrumb consistency. Stir in the sugar and bind into a stiff dough with the beaten egg, adding a little water if necessary. To make the almond paste, mix together the ground almonds and sugars. Bind with the egg yolk into a stiff paste, and flavour to taste with the lemon juice. Roll into 16 balls using sugared fingers. Roll the dough into a sausage shape and divide into 16 equal portions. Shape into balls on a floured board and flatten slightly. Place a ball of almond paste in the centre of each bun and gather the edges together over it. Turn upside down and place on a greased baking sheet. Brush the buns with beaten egg white and sprinkle with flaked almonds. Bake in a preheated hot oven at 425°F or Gas mark 7 for 15 minutes or until well risen and golden brown. Cool on a wire tray.

Cheese Scones

8 oz. plain flour   ½ tsp. salt   1 tsp. dry mustard
4 tsp. baking powder   2 oz. butter   1 egg, beaten
3-4 oz. mature Cheddar cheese, grated
¼ pint milk

Sift the flour, salt, mustard and baking powder into a mixing bowl. Cut the butter in to the flour and rub in to a breadcrumb consistency. Mix in the grated cheese. Beat the egg with half the liquid and stir into the dry ingredients. Work into a soft dough adding more liquid if necessary. Turn on to a well-floured board and roll out lightly until ¾ inch thick. Cut out rounds with a 2½ inch cutter. Place on a warmed baking sheet. Brush with milk and sprinkle with grated cheese. Bake in a preheated hot oven at 425°F or Gas mark 7 for 10 to 15 minutes until well risen and golden. Cool on a wire tray.

Rich Malt Loaf

1 oz. fresh yeast	¼ pint warm water
1 lb. flour	1 tsp. salt
2-3 oz. sultanas	4 oz. malt extract
1 tbsp. black treacle	1 oz. butter

Dissolve the yeast in the warm water. Leave for 10 minutes or until frothy. Sift the flour and salt into a warm bowl and mix in the sultanas. Heat the malt, treacle and butter gently in a small pan until melted, then cool slightly. Stir the yeast liquid and malt mixture into the dry ingredients and mix to a soft dough, adding more water if necessary. Turn the dough on to a floured board and knead until firm and elastic. Split the dough in half, shape and put into two greased 1 lb. loaf tins. Cover and leave to prove until the dough rises to the top of the tins. Malt dough rises slowly so this may take up to 2 hours. Bake in the centre of a preheated moderately hot oven at 400°F or Gas mark 6 for 30 to 40 minutes. When cooked, remove the loaves, brush the tops with sugar syrup and return to the oven for 2 minutes. Cool on a wire tray.

Ginger and Raisin Cake

8 oz. flour	4 oz. butter
8 oz. treacle	1 large egg, beaten
3 oz. sugar	8 oz. raisins
3 level tsp. ground ginger	¼ pint milk
1 level tsp. bicarbonate of soda	2 tbsp. lemon juice

Butter and line the base a 7 inch round cake tin. Warm the treacle and sugar gently until thoroughly melted and then cool. Sift the flour with the bicarbonate of soda and ground ginger into a bowl. Rub in the butter and stir in the raisins. Form a well in the centre of the dry ingredients and add the cooled treacle, egg, lemon juice and milk. Mix thoroughly. Pour into the cake tin and bake in the oven at 325°F or Gas mark 3 for about 1¼ hours. Test with a skewer which should come out clean when the cake is cooked. Cool in the tin for 15 minutes before turning out on to a wire rack. When cold, wrap and store in an airtight container for at least 2 days before eating.

Drop Scones

8 oz. self-raising flour	½ pint milk
1 level tsp. caster sugar	1-2 oz. melted butter
½ level tsp. salt	1 egg

Sift flour and salt into bowl. Add sugar then mix to a smooth batter with the egg and half the milk. Stir in the remaining milk. Lightly brush a large griddle iron, or heavy frying pan with melted butter and heat. Drop small rounds of scone mixture from a tablespoon into the pan. Cook over a moderate heat until bubbles show on the scone surface. Carefully turn over with a palette knife and cook for further 2 minutes. Repeat until all the mixture is used up. Keep scones warm in a folded tea-towel. Serve immediately with butter and jam.

Honey Cake with Ginger

8 oz. flour	1 tsp. bicarbonate of soda
1 tsp. ground ginger	4 oz. stem ginger, chopped
2 oz. caster sugar	$\frac{1}{4}$ pint milk
4 oz. butter	1 egg, beaten

2 oz. clear honey

Line the base of a 6 inch cake tin. Sift the flour and ground ginger into a mixing bowl. Cut the butter into the flour and rub in to a breadcrumb consistency. Mix in the sugar and stem ginger. Dissolve the bicarbonate of soda in half the milk and stir into the honey. Make a well in the dry ingredients and stir in the milk mixture and beaten egg. Mix thoroughly to a soft dropping consistency, adding more milk if required. Pour into the tin and smooth the top. Bake in the centre of a preheated moderate oven at 325°F or Gas mark 3 for about 1 hour, until cooked and golden. Allow to cool slightly, remove from the tin and turn onto a wire tray.

Plain Buns

8 oz. flour	1 egg, beaten
1 tsp. baking powder	2-3 oz. sugar
Pinch of salt	3 fl.oz. milk
3 oz. butter	2 tsp. grated lemon rind

Sift the flour, salt and baking powder into a mixing bowl and add the grated lemon rind. Cut the butter into the flour, rub in to a breadcrumb consistency and mix in the sugar thoroughly. Using a fork, stir in the egg and sufficient milk to give a stiff consistency. Divide the mixture into greased bun tins and bake near the top of a preheated hot oven at 425 to 450°F or Gas mark 7 to 8 for 10 to 15 minutes. Cool on a wire tray.

Gingerbread

4 oz. butter   2 oz. golden syrup   6 oz. black treacle   ¼ pint milk
2 eggs, beaten   7 oz. flour   1 oz. ground almonds   2 tsp. ground ginger
1 tsp. ground cinnamon   ½ tsp. ground nutmeg   ¼ tsp. ground cloves
1 tsp. bicarbonate of soda   2 oz. stem ginger, chopped   2 oz. sultanas
1 oz. chopped candied peel

FROSTING:
8 oz. icing sugar   Lemon juice to mix   Crystallised ginger

Grease and line the base of a round 7–8 inch cake tin or a square 6–7 inch tin. Heat the fat, syrup and treacle gently until melted, then stir in the milk. Cool slightly and mix in the eggs. Sift the flour, almonds, ground ginger, cinnamon, nutmeg, cloves and soda into a mixing bowl. Make a well in the centre and mix in the liquid. Beat into a smooth batter. Add half the remaining ingredients and fold in. Repeat with the rest of the ingredients. Pour into the prepared tin and bake in the centre of a cool oven at 300°F or Gas mark 2, for up to 2 hours, until a skewer inserted comes out clean. Allow to cool slightly before turning out on to a wire tray to cool thoroughly. When cold, mix the unsifted icing sugar with just enough lemon juice to make a spreading consistency. Spread over the top of the cake. Decorate with a few pieces of chopped crystallised ginger.

Lemon Cake

**6 oz. butter   6 oz. caster sugar   Finely grated rind and juice of 1½ lemons
3 eggs, beaten   6 oz. self-raising flour   3 oz. icing sugar
10 fl.oz. double cream**

Grease and line the base of two 8 inch sandwich tins. Whisk the butter and sugar together in a bowl until pale and fluffy, then beat in the grated lemon rind. Gradually add the beaten eggs and mix well. Sift the flour and gently fold it into the cake mixture. Divide the mixture between the two tins, and level the surface. Bake in the oven at 350°F or Gas mark 4 for about 25 minutes, until well risen and firm to the touch. Leave the cakes to cool slightly in the tins, then turn out and stand one cake on top of the other on a plate. Pierce through both layers of cake with a skewer. Gently heat the lemon juice and icing sugar in a pan, stir until the sugar dissolves, then bring almost to boiling point. Slowly pour the hot syrup all over the top of the cakes allowing time for it to soak through and be absorbed. Cover with cling film and leave for 1 hour. Whip the cream until stiff. Place one cake on a plate, spread with the whipped cream, and top with the second cake. Dust the top of the cake with icing sugar.

Crispy Coconut Cookies

6 oz. self-raising flour	5 oz. butter
3 oz. caster sugar	2 oz. shredded coconut
2 oz. desiccated coconut	2 eggs, separated

Mix together the flour, desiccated coconut and sugar. Cut the butter into the mixture and rub in to a breadcrumb consistency. Beat the egg yolks and stir into the mixture. Knead thoroughly into a stiff smooth dough. Put in a cool place for 30 minutes. Roll out thinly on a floured board and prick all over and cut into 2 inch rounds. Place the rounds on a greased baking sheet a little apart to allow for spreading. Brush the biscuits with beaten egg white and cover with shredded coconut. Bake in a preheated moderate oven at 350°F or Gas mark 4 for 15 minutes until set and golden. Cool on a wire tray and store in an airtight tin.

Shortbread

8 oz. flour   **4 oz. ground rice**
4 oz. caster sugar   **8 oz. unsalted butter**
Pinch of salt

Sift the flour and ground rice, sugar and salt, into a mixing bowl. Soften the butter slightly, cut it up and rub it into the dry ingredients with your fingers. When it starts to bind, gather it together with one hand into a ball. Knead it on a lightly floured board until it is a soft, smooth and pliable dough. Place an 8 inch flan ring on a greased baking tray and put in the dough. Press it out evenly to fit the ring. With the back of a knife, mark it into 6 or 8 triangles. Prick with a fork. Chill for at least 1 hour before baking. Bake in the centre of a preheated cool oven at 300°F or Gas mark 2 for 45 minutes to 1 hour until it is pale but still soft. Remove from the oven and leave to cool before removing the ring, then dust lightly with caster sugar. When cold cut into the triangles and store in an airtight tin.

Fruited Scones

8 oz. flour   Pinch of salt   ½ tsp. cream of tartar
½ tsp. bicarbonate of soda   1½ oz. butter
1 oz. caster sugar   2 oz. sultanas   ¼ pint buttermilk

Sift the flour, salt, cream of tartar and bicarbonate of soda into a mixing bowl. Cut the butter into the flour and rub in to a breadcrumb consistency. Mix in the sugar and sultanas. Stir in enough liquid to give a soft dough. Knead lightly on a floured board until smooth. Roll out lightly until about ½ inch thick and cut into rounds with a 2 inch cutter. Place the scones on a warmed floured baking sheet. Brush the tops with a little milk. Bake near the top of a preheated hot oven at 450°F or Gas mark 8 for about 10 minutes until well risen and golden. Cool on a wire tray.

Sultana Cake

8 oz. flour	8 oz. soft brown sugar
8 oz. plain wholemeal flour	8 oz. sultanas
6 oz. butter	1 egg, beaten
2 level tsp. mixed spice	About ½ pint milk
1 level tsp. bicarbonate of soda	Granulated sugar

Grease and line the base of an 8 inch square cake tin. Sift the plain flour with the mixed spice and bicarbonate into a mixing bowl and stir in the wholemeal flour. Rub in the butter until the mixture resembles fine breadcrumbs and stir in the sugar and sultanas. Make a well in the centre of the dry ingredients and add the egg and milk. Beat gently until well mixed and of a soft dropping consistency, adding extra milk if necessary. Pour into the prepared tin. Scatter granulated sugar over the cake. Bake in the oven at 325°F or Gas mark 3 for about 1 hour 40 minutes until cooked (test with a fine skewer). Turn out and cool on a wire rack.

Coconut and Cherry Cake

9 oz. self-raising flour
4 oz. butter
½ level tsp. salt
3 oz. desiccated coconut
4 oz. caster sugar
4 oz. glacé cherries, finely chopped
8 fl.oz. milk
2 eggs, beaten
1 oz. shredded coconut

Grease and line the base of a 2¼ pint loaf tin. In a bowl mix the flour and salt and rub in the butter. Stir in the coconut, sugar and cherries. Whisk together the eggs and milk and beat in to the other ingredients. Pour the mixture into the prepared tin, smoothing the top and scatter over the shredded coconut. Bake in the oven at 350°F or Gas mark 4 for about 1¼ hours, covering with foil after 40 minutes. Turn out on to a wire rack and leave to cool.

Boiled Cake

8 oz. plain flour	4 oz. sultanas
4 oz. sugar	3 oz. golden syrup
4 oz. currants	1 tsp. bicarbonate of soda
4 oz. butter	1 tsp. ground ginger
¼ pint water	1 tsp. mixed spices
	1 egg, beaten

Dissolve the syrup, sugar and butter in the water in a saucepan over moderate heat. Add the dried fruit and boil gently for 10 minutes. Pour into a mixing bowl to cool. Meanwhile, grease a round 6 inch cake tin and line the base with greaseproof paper. Sift the flour with the bicarbonate of soda and spices. Stir it into the cooled boiled mixture and mix in the egg. Turn the mixture into the prepared tin and bake in the centre of a preheated moderate oven at 350°F or Gas mark 4 for about 1½ hours or until a skewer comes out clean. Allow the cake to cool slightly. Turn out on to a wire tray to cool thoroughly.

Rich Seed Cake

4 oz. flour
4 oz. butter
4 oz. caster sugar
2 large eggs, separated
1 tbsp. whisky
Caraway seeds

¼ tsp. baking powder
¼ tsp. grated nutmeg
2 oz. blanched almonds, shredded
2 oz. candied orange peel, chopped
1 oz. candied citron peel, chopped
Granulated sugar

Line the sides and base of a round 6 inch cake tin. Cream the butter and sugar until light and fluffy. Gradually beat in the egg yolks. Whisk the egg whites until stiff, and fold in alternately with the flour, sifted with the baking powder and nutmeg. Fold in the almonds, candied peel and whisky. Turn into the prepared tin and sprinkle with the caraway seeds and granulated sugar. Bake in the centre of a preheated moderate oven at 325°F or Gas mark 3 for 1½ hours until cooked through and golden (test with a skewer). Allow the cake to cool slightly. Turn out on to a wire tray, remove the lining paper and leave to cool completely.

Angel Cake

4 oz. flour   **½ tsp. cream of tartar**
6 oz. caster sugar   **6 fl.oz. egg whites**
½ tsp. vanilla essence

Sift the flour and sugar together 3 to 4 times to get plenty of air into the mix. Beat the egg whites until foaming, add the cream of tartar and whisk until stiff but not dry. Add the flour and sugar on to the whisked egg whites carefully, a little at a time, then fold in the vanilla essence. Turn the mixture into 7 inch angel cake tin. Bake in a preheated moderate oven at 325°F or Gas mark 3 for 1 hour or until a skewer inserted comes out clean. Remove from the oven, allow to cool slightly and invert on to a wire tray. Leave until quite cold before turning out of the tin. This is a sweet cake and it is best to choose a sharp filling. Slice the cake across into three and spread the slices with lemon curd. Re-assemble the cake and spread with lemon glacé icing.

Lemon Biscuits

8 oz. self-raising flour	4 oz. caster or icing sugar, sifted
6 oz. butter	1 level tsp. finely grated lemon rind
Pinch of salt	1 egg, beaten

Sift the flour and salt into a bowl, then rub in the butter until the mixture resembles fine breadcrumbs. Add the sugar and lemon rind, and mix to a stiff dough with the beaten egg. Turn out on to lightly floured work surface. Knead gently until smooth. Wrap in cling film and chill in the refrigerator for 30 minutes. Roll the dough out fairly thinly. Cut into rounds with a 2 inch plain biscuit cutter. Place on a buttered baking tray and prick each biscuit with a fork. Bake in a preheated oven at 350°F or Gas mark 4 for about 12 to 15 minutes, until pale golden. Leave for a few minutes, then cool on a wire rack. Store in an airtight tin.

Marmalade Cake

8 oz. self-raising flour	1 oz. lard or vegetable fat
1 tbsp. golden syrup	3 oz. margarine
1 tbsp. marmalade	3 oz. sugar
2 eggs	Mixed fruit
Vanilla essence	Pinch of salt

Cream the sugar and fat very thoroughly together, add the salt, syrup and marmalade. Beat the eggs. Sift the flour and add to the mixture alternately with the eggs, beating well. Stir in the fruit (sultanas, raisins, currants, chopped dates, glacé cherries, mixed peel), according to taste and availability and flavouring. Bake in a well-greased, unlined tin in a moderate oven at 375°F or Gas mark 5 for about 1 hour 20 minutes.

Ring Doughnuts

12 oz. self-raising flour	2 oz. caster sugar
¼ level tsp. salt	1 egg
½ level tsp. cinnamon	¼ pint milk
½ level tsp. mixed spice	Oil for frying
4 oz. butter	Extra caster sugar

Sift the flour, salt, cinnamon and mixed spice into bowl. Rub in the butter finely and add the caster sugar. Beat the egg with the milk and add to the dry ingredients. Mix to a soft dough with a knife, turn out on to a lightly floured board. Knead quickly until smooth. Roll out to ½ inch thickness. Cut into rounds with 2 inch biscuit cutter and remove centres with 1 inch cutter. Re-roll the spare dough and cut into more rings. Fry, a few at a time, in hot fat or oil for 2 to 3 minutes, turning once. Remove from pan. Drain thoroughly on soft kitchen paper. Toss in caster sugar. Serve while still warm.

Dundee Cake

6 oz. flour	3 oz. mixed peel (chopped)
4 oz. butter	6 oz. brown sugar
1 tsp. baking powder	Pinch of salt
3 oz. currants	Pinch of mixed spice
6 oz. sultanas	3 eggs

Almonds

Cream the butter and sugar until light and fluffy. Add the beaten eggs gradually, and then all the dry ingredients, sifted and mixed together. Stir in the fruit and put the mixture into a cake tin, lined with greaseproof paper. Scatter the almonds on the top and bake in a moderate oven at 375°F or Gas mark 5 for about 2¼ hours.

Oat Crunchies

1 oz. flour	6 oz. wholemeal flour
1 oz. medium oatmeal	1 level tsp. baking powder
3 oz. butter	1 level tsp. salt
5 tbsp. milk	

Sift the flour, baking powder and salt into a bowl. Add the wholemeal flour and oatmeal. Rub in the butter and then mix to a firm dough with the milk, adding slowly until the correct consistency is achieved. Roll out on floured work surface until ½ inch thick. Cut into squares. Place on buttered baking tray and brush with milk. Bake in the oven at 400°F or Gas mark 6 for about 10 minutes, until just golden. Cool and store in an airtight container.

Rock Cakes

12 oz. flour	4 oz. currants
1 tsp. baking powder	1 oz. chopped peel
3 oz. sugar	3 oz. butter
1 egg	Pinch of mixed spice
Milk	Nutmeg

Sieve the flour into a bowl and rub in the butter. Add all the remaining dry ingredients and mix thoroughly. Beat the egg and add it and a little milk for consistency, but the mixture must be quite dry. Stir with a spoon, keeping a rough texture. Put little heaps on a floured baking tray and bake in a moderate oven at 375°F or Gas mark 5 for 15 minutes.

Meringues

2 egg whites
4 oz. caster sugar
5 fl.oz. fresh double cream

Line two baking sheets with non-stick baking paper. Whisk the egg whites until stiff. Add the caster sugar a tablespoon at a time, whisking well for about 1 minute after each addition. Pipe or spoon 10 to 12 rounds or oblongs of the meringue on to the non-stick paper. Bake in the oven at 225°F or Gas mark ½ for about 2 to 3 hours, changing the position of the trays half way through the cooking. Cool on a wire rack. Whip the fresh cream until stiff and use to sandwich together the meringue shells.

Custard Tarts

6 oz. sweet shortcrust pastry
¾ pint milk
2 eggs

2-3 teaspoons sugar
¾ tsp. vanilla essence
Grated nutmeg

Roll out the pastry thinly and line greased tart tins. Bake blind in a preheated moderately hot oven at 400°F or Gas mark 6 for 12 to 15 minutes until set but not brown, then remove from the oven. Lower the heat to 325°F or Gas mark 3. Warm the milk over a low heat and meanwhile beat the eggs and sugar together. Stir the warm milk gradually into the beaten eggs and flavour with the vanilla. Strain the custard through a sieve into the partially baked cases. Sprinkle the tops with grated nutmeg and return the tarts to the centre of the oven for 15 to 20 minutes until the custard is set. Serve cold.

Butterscotch Brownies

2 oz. butter   8 oz. soft brown sugar   1 egg, beaten
¾ tsp. vanilla essence   2 oz. flour
1 tsp. baking powder   ½ tsp. salt
4 oz. chopped mixed hazelnuts and walnuts

Grease and line the base of a shallow 8 inch square tin. Melt the butter in a saucepan over gentle heat, then mix in the sugar and stir until dissolved. Cool slightly and beat in the egg and vanilla essence. Sift the flour together with baking powder and salt and mix in thoroughly. Stir in the nuts and pour into the prepared tin. Bake in a preheated moderately hot oven at 375°F or Gas mark 5 about 30 minutes or until set, but not hard. Cut into squares while still hot, then allow to cool in the tin. When cold, lift out carefully and store in an airtight tin or container.

METRIC CONVERSIONS

The weights, measures and oven temperatures used in the preceding recipes can be easily converted to their metric equivalents. The conversions listed below are only approximate, having been rounded up or down as may be appropriate.

Weights

Avoirdupois	Metric
1 oz.	just under 30 grams
4 oz. (¼ lb.)	app. 115 grams
8 oz. (½ lb.)	app. 230 grams
1 lb.	454 grams

Liquid Measures

Imperial	Metric
1 tablespoon (liquid only)	20 millilitres
1 fl. oz.	app. 30 millilitres
1 gill (¼ pt.)	app. 145 millilitres
½ pt.	app. 285 millilitres
1 pt.	app. 570 millilitres
1 qt.	app. 1.140 litres

Oven Temperatures

	°Fahrenheit	Gas Mark	°Celsius
Slow	300	2	150
	325	3	170
Moderate	350	4	180
	375	5	190
	400	6	200
Hot	425	7	220
	450	8	230
	475	9	240

Flour as specified in these recipes refers to plain flour unless otherwise described.